Come an

by Nicholas Spencer
illustrated by Jo Parry

Come and play
with the marbles.
We have lots of marbles.

Come and play
with the mud.
We have lots of mud.

Come and play
with the kites.
We have lots of kites.

Come and read
the books.
We have lots of books.

Come and sit
on the bench.
We have lots of room.

Come and eat
the melon.
We have lots of melon.

Come and play with us!